FON

Fondue

A. K. BLAKEMORE

First published in 2018
by Offord Road Books

www.offordroadbooks.co.uk
@OffordRoadBooks

Typeset by Martha Sprackland
Printed in the UK by TJ International

ISBN 978–1–999–93043–1

1 3 5 7 9 10 8 6 4 2

O•R•B

for Sheila Blakemore

Contents

She never undertook to know
What death with love should have to do;
Nor has she e'er yet understood
Why to show love she should shed blood;
Yet though she cannot tell you why,
She can love, and she can die.

Richard Crashaw, *A Hymn to the Name*
and Honour of Admirable Saint Teresa

my sex

enter breakfast truck, the bluebottles
performing obsequies to marbled bacon

enter girl with manacles. enter
so damn adorable. he likes small fuckdoll.

girl who looks plaintively at porcelain
salt and pepper shakers shaped
like kittens sleeping, intertwined. enter
desolation beside a pinstripe spider plant enter
knowing how to dress your pear-shape history
history, and after you follow, with a bucket
and a mop – or words to that effect.

enter girl who applies the cooling gel. enter
the Tate Modern to see Yayoi Kusama's
I Am Here But Nothing which *please* you
cannot photograph like when
i found out there was a fetish for everything sexuality
seemed like a great leveller. enter nothing
too weird to enter, biking, amused savage
tender repetitions of toilet cubicle graffiti.

enter *Fathers in the Clouds ('99)*
enter my sex like act not gender and other songs
that make me cry my sex sometimes ballet shoes
both the stones in the pockets of my coat
and the welcoming cold river.

prelude

i watched a porn
in which a woman pushed her lips to the fractal stream
of a hosepipe aimed at a car window.

the man with the hosepipe was wearing overalls
beside a privet line of rosebushes, parti-coloured by the
   spray –
a striped umbrella, a jug of pale lemonade.

it seemed so *actual*
the scene was poignant

and then i wondered where you were.

ex

persistent beloved, hear my sad emesis
when you shave over exotic sinks.

look for me once i'm gone,
like the tiredest star, silver skin crackling
with premature age.

look!
i'm hurling dead light back across the universe
for you.

scorpion

i want you
like a scorpion down my shirt.
struggling through life
toward me only

a scorpion, and a white mouse
caught in human hair.

if you are prepared to live cheaply
i might show you alternate lucre.

in a friendly way i will get drunk
and call you *a sick fuck*

say *we needn't leave late*
if you're tired. i see you

watching
as i shake the petals from my damp umbrella
like anyone is looking at my shoes.

saturday night friends

the dealer comes to order
and morning is a bird trapped in the curtains.

the first time he talks earnestly about his prescriptions.
my heart and lungs a painful texture in the somnolent glow of
our mutual history as a painted silk –

the hidden dredgers on the river,
crust punks shooting up, the sepulchritude
of the endless grasses on Blackheath in the many summers.

smoking in the violet grounds of the hospital,
like dubious pricks, as we did –

neither in your darkest hour
nor at this moment of political chaos
can you turn to me

but i will never look for ways to humiliate you
and in this sense i am your friend.

fondue

this is a poem about my mouth
intended to draw attention
to my mouth.

demure – consider me
a woman on a first date, strawberry speared
on a miniature fork, poised to dip –

with this mouth i will teach you what it means
to live

without fear of contaminants.

art locusts

brought home to participate
in independent film-making: the actor is
to strip to the waist and weep
cornstarch –

in phase
gregaria –
the locusts climb and i can't
stop watching:

those tiny automatic horses
of Romanov toy-rooms, taupe
& glitter.

our pinched art weighs heavy
on their evolution.

ice machine

will you accept this as proof someone
else has existed fully? thought

he has an aura
the colour of dried blood, even
said these words out loud.

and here we are. thirty degrees outside,
fans respirating with the scent of dusty artificial flowers
and gluten, a touch on the hand
like a hotel ice machine –

somehow thrilling
and American.

when my boyfriend spanks me
my inner feminist weeps

reading Proust
Swann's Way
the Moncrieff and Kilmartin translation
impressing boys

insect-bitten legs swollen out
to cloisonne, pure coral horn –

poor Mlle. Vinteuil! performative sadism
belies her good heart.
and the wasps *botanising*.

i hate poems where something is realised
on a holiday on a rope swing

i realise nothing
and do so hate to explain
i know i don't deserve to be hurt

later the cheap beer in the bar off the Old Town square
and the life-size wooden gypsy 'wench'
with the varnish worn off her breasts

like a talisman
of male predictability –

in bed i place your hands saying
you like it like this don't you
you like it here

sadism

at home i am unknotting the yellow cardigan
i used to bind your wrists last night.

dry and cold and eager
like a maybug the morning of nuptial flight.

soft drink

my desires are so
ultimately bourgeois –

mainly you standing by a window
with a soft drink in your hand

beneath the curling red paws
of the neighbours' rose-bushes.

Andrea Dworkin

i can do it in a room alone
and nobody can stop me. i think of you
at the bar when from behind and it is
great refreshment –
gin and tonic sweating on my nipple
through a thin white t-shirt
or the wave of delicious pollution at a sun-lit bus stop.
o Andrea –

so much of what has happened
(molested by the unknown, internally examined)
seems like it would be treated as a metaphor by other,
    larger hands

the ones that seek to reassure us.

gums

what would it mean to you if i said *mother*
at the kitchen table? Schopenhauer?

dentists are beginning to know you now.
teeth are autobiography – the orphan genre –
a fixed address & useful hardware. it's morbid but i stayed
   up late
to read about the victims of Jeffrey Dahmer.

how sad –
to be the one who is not reported missing, resolved
to filed record, a few unseated vertebrae. a drifter.
predictably had nightmares
of a different serial killer, an injection of perplexity
direct to the brain. i want you to describe the pain

like a hair is caught between the two front teeth
or a filament, aflame.
fig 1: you bite the hem of the wedding dress and they all
   come clean
away. when you think about them, teeth are odd – these
   chromium exposed
parts on, not of, our bodies. but not as odd as your mouth
   would look without them –
like a blood orange, split and
dripping . . .

i like to touch the sides
of your face, a little below the
the ears, just after you have shaved.

II

i'd follow you through the mirror to a dreamscape made up
of calorific pinks and corals. proper ayahuasca shit, please
   let me
sit beside

and touch your gorgeous feet
the whole trip –
and when the stepped pyramid opens
like a grin, we'll be there, by Dahmer's altar –

the black vinyl shower curtain and dicks preserved
in jars. i'll hold you close and tell you the story about the
   ladybird
that bit my finger in the park.

Perseus

the body – taken whole –
he pulled into the surf like a dismembered leg.
her breasts still lovely, her green seahawk wings
ophidian cutlery.

he and the head
would wake at the same time,
with the same infection. a drop
falling from the slack mouth, like the liquid
sometimes wept from the centre of a flower.
where it fell on his boots, it melted through the leather.

even covered or tied in a sack
it's bad, carrying a thing like that. he flew above
a burning orchard. kept seeing birds
eating other birds.

grandmother's cat

my grandmother's cat is ugly
because he's always been that way:

the woollen wrists,
scapolite eye unhooked
in quasi-mystical disputation –

but he is also beautiful and this because i hold him
in very high esteem.

Baader-Meinhof

excuse me
i couldn't help noticing you
from over there and
thinking

i just took the first step toward dying
for something i
believe in —

Wolf Blass

never say
the best of summer's gone –

a cloud in the belly
of your wine. i haven't
thought about a boy like this before –

the combed-forward hair, the way i like
to watch him touch himself, see him lay down
in a pool of sunshine

with just such an attitude
of rapt self-care.

spanish plume

the city
held tight in spanish plume –
a beggar outside the skatewear shop
rolls his trousers up an artificial leg.

people like my boyfriend
worry they'll weaponise their defects
against beloveds. the edible silver
of their hot night-sweats –

how
he soothes me

how by stirring, shifts the weight
he'll never care for. then

(most consoling certainty)
how stroking makes it hard –

Fountayn Road

it could've been a corpse in the car. certainly
he had been on something all day, his gums mauve
like a brachycephalic puppy's.

mention it again
how i am a child harpist

and everyone else and their sufferings
are strings.

nymphs

i am a dumb receiver
walking back through the mist with eggs
and a sprig of pussywillow.

our new home has cockroaches.
an exterminator came –

with a tattoo of a rearing scorpion
and his daughter's name in Tamil on his forearm.

it's smart how the poisoned gel spreads through the colony
by cannibalism. he explains that they will eat their family,
that the poison will spread faster that way.

Gregor

i attempt to conceal my disgust as you draw your squat
   body up to the dish of milk.

then hovering, i half expect the drop
of a fibrous needle.

lifting away, you point yourself at me –
dark-eyed, somehow
accusatory.

i lead you to the bed and hold your hardened forewings
   against my body, a melanoid baby.

the *real you* would laugh if you could see me . . . like the
   believers
who rub their quilted nightgowns against the stone of
   unction,
feeling out a lay line –

some way to make things right with Him. the him
   there is God.
i think you are elaborated memory.

complaints:
the silence of your over-wintering.

anxiety makes your legs emit dark fluid
and the bedroom smells of dead leaves.
i try to read.

Boy with rare skin condition finds new best friend –
a dog with the same condition.

the mattress springs are throbbing
beneath your many, dormant hearts.

house cat

sunday
and where we've loved it's burning.

the house cat rests her chin on the sill
and you ask her if she can smell the bluebells and
daisies neophyte
in the window box –

rooks' nests, a bailiff
whistling.

sometimes you even bend
say adorably

hey little one
hey fluff

how dare you walk away from me

the drunk wives

last night we rang around confirming
we'd dream of a visibly unwashed god
and tapestried shoe lost by a cycle-path, then keening,
flung our avian wrists at the breasts of pomaded architects.

now the morning.
what magnificent glassware we drink from, blink through,
in chemise, with the poise of an equilux, at gardens
   threaded with in-laws
who admire the chinese foxgloves.

Cupid

bring me
into the hush of an urn –
a stroll of the hopeless lights
by our expensive home.

blessed my Lord and Saviour
with his loose waistband
and poor circulation –

it is life dancing
in a slackening grip.

at this point staying up
all night to talk about yourself
loses

all utopian savour.

poem

i want to be so pretty that i'm
so pretty that people will say
she's so pretty it's like
annoying

The Book of the Dead

mother,
i have fallen in with some bad days.
i'm sure time would pass more quickly if i could commit
to a regular pattern of aggressive masturbation.

as it is
i groom it – pick
at flesh & use up oxygen.

i watched a documentary about Tutankhamun
in which they carried out a ground-breaking 3D autopsy.

dead at nineteen.
Köhler disease, Malaria Tropica –

and among the treasures of his tomb, innumerable
walking-sticks &

an unused meteorite dagger.

a body

remainder
of the rain had slid
into hollows in the bitumen.

it was probably a fox
but so dead it had become ur-animal, un-
named.

white teeth in flat, blackened muzzle.

it was so hideous, so
un-
purposefully slung
across the stained orthopaedic mattress

i hoped no one would remove it
sentimentally

i wanted to show it to you.

mephedrone

I

she called me from by the river
but all i could hear was her red hair.
she'd lost so much by then and

i was interested in how
girls *construct themselves* again –

II

read a news story about a dealer
putting a kitchen knife through a python's head
because he was owed money.

how fast would it happen
under a serpent-weight?

as a way to go about things,
undeniably poetic.

i think this was in Newport
the empty tank hot as blood with
directionless heat-lamps

III

it was wonderful sometimes,
a black meadow, your heart

a heraldic symbol
floating somewhere
in front of you

impatient
to slot back
where it belonged

IV

smooth leg and
gold-plated astrological anklet –

as we smoked out the skylight
she said

if you feel sick you probably
should just be sick. yes.

V

no responsible person would walk
down that street alone at
that time –

the drips from the railway bridge
became the tappings
of something
incarnate –

something tall. a man
who carried a metal-tipped cane.

clearance

on the street we feel a certain way
like adept at avoiding the question, maybe
having sewed slogan patches
on our jeans.

the market
is so meat-affiliated:

imagine that mouth-feel!
the epithelial curves
of wet broilers,

laundry bags,
estate clearance:
a miniature Shire horse
with mock-pearl hooves. i lose your ring
at a table heaped with old viscose sweaters.

lovers

i was frustrated by
the way he received fellatio.

that very blonde underarm –

with the passivity
of a teddy bear of a dog –
how
(tight-clasping memory!)

no one was allowed to hurt him
but me.

bean

listening to hard rock.
leaving the satin belt of my red kimono
dropped on the threshold of the master bedroom.

i raised myself slowly
like a vine

from this square-toed soul.

our town

the dead rat was uninjured.
rigor mortis had set in, freezing the tail to a loop about
the circumference of my forearm.
probably

it had eaten poison. when it rains the snails
come out in their tiaras
of liquid and

at night i saw a car with blue
under-lights parked
outside the restaurant. another place sells fruit loaves and
secondhand bridesmaids' dresses.

i don't know where to buy khat yet. salvia
i do. ask me about my tattoos.
red-and-white striped

tube-top. heart-shaped padlock.
i didn't notice him putting his hand
there. it was raining.

but hold me
like something that shakes
when it goes unheld. you've trained
your body not to take up the space
it ought to take –

and everyone else we've ever met
would die if they came to this place.

Christmas

i sit by the fern
in the station waiting room, and later recover
my copy of *The Bell Jar*
from the oak bookcase
from the oak catalogue.

she reserves the psychodrama
for birthdays. but i came to your little town
carrying my guile to the curry place like
a spasming doll.

but where *did* i spend the money?
drugs? Acne?

precious little on socialising
with other actual human beings, father
says.

leather

intentions
seemed so concrete by the estuary –

next to the water
(a dark flesh, like leather)

taking deep
malt-works' lotos smell.

they shit along the greensward,
all shameless white scars
of neck. there

like if Tom of Finland
had made swans –

mauve tails
for tongues –

primed
to cusp a girlhood
in ex-cathedra feather.

making it in the art world

can't say if i skip meals
to keep my costs down or
that second rib showing –

like Jennifer Lawrence post-
photoshop, all
authentic pale lip and

i miss the days when the heat would rise
from someone else's home
below mine

dust

a handful of small skeletons
having a sand-like consistency

collected in the shade
of the old angle-poise lamp.
i want to lay them on slides
and see a revivification

performed
in a flush of vegetable dye –

you sleep beside / just outside
my little circle of light

arm under my vest
docile as a smoke ring.

Lilith

there is no intellectual pleasure.

i caught the large moth
with my bare hands –

like a kiss blown
from black marshland, that
old bad mama

storyboard for a conceptual horror movie

I

from the car, he sees two young girls playing tennis
in black thermals. floodlit, rapt —

they are identical twins.
they may be beautiful.

in cursive, red-on-black,
the words flash:

the front of heaven
was full of fiery shapes.

II

the elderly dowager
holds a red rose to her mouth.

this is a subtle visual reference
to *Achilles Mourning the Death of Patroclus* —
the painting by Cy Twombly
he saw hanging in the Louvre.

III

scene
of brutal glossectomy
(footage of ripe avocado, inexpertly de-stoned.)

on a country walk in mid–february
our heroes find a hollowful of blood.
their discovery is all the more menacing
because unlike the puddles of rain that spot
the rural path around it, this hollowful of blood
has not frozen over.

probably foxes, or

wildlife,
says one.

amateur

to listen
to their conversation
i became a blue silk fan

spread high on the wall
of the chinese restaurant –

& then
the same beneath him.

February 13th

love is . . . slowed down
like an ice-dancing championship replay –

bodies touched by a horde
of lights – the costumes
tipped in radium paint.

this is the moment i feel i have lost you –
when there is a heart slipping out of the race.

our love, through the marbled end-papers –
our love, biting through the bone like a mechanical bird –

so touched always by misunderstood human gestures.

southern gothic

riding trains makes me think about death.
not mine, you understand,
but my father's.

the specificity. sun scrapes along the half-spent cloud,
    union jacks sinuate on satellite dishes.

England –
and just enough blue sky
to make a noose.

i'll walk around the two-bed with my attention turned
    to chores unfinished –
mow the lawn, throw my cigarette ends at the cat
who comes to shit in the daffodil patch.

walking through mourning days
of a nitrous quality

with the calm and self-possession
of a knife-carrier.

Tiergarten

and a short walk further along the Landwehr canal from where Rosa Luxemberg
was pulled from the spring-thawed waters like a white shoe, a vulture perched on a stump
with wings radiate to diabolical span.

i'm sorry. it was presumptuous to call it a vulture at all
when it could have been a winged man.

mermaids

the fossil record indicates they were once numerous, and filled the depths
with bursting protein cases like tributary oleanders about the rusted airelons
of passenger jets. the only fish that understood leap days, they would mouth
at one another how

they always felt fraudulent around death.

bedspread

my pale pink bedspread is edged with glass beads so that i
    feel like
i have lined my chamber with the skins of the thousand
    rag dolls
i have slain.

i am a tiny soft-lipped khan
scratching my tongue with a flamingo bone!

i can practically feel
the smartly-trousered knee
of the hetero Kray twin pressing hard between my breasts

when i roll over in the night and
the glass beads make a sound like

duchess duchess duchess . . .

samaritans

falling in love with the boy dragging
old bits of wood and broken pallets
through the green adolescent limbs
of wheat

liking how he lit fires, must be
constantly in the presence of fire

and my readiness to scream
when he was around –
to test that space within.

later i was referred to a therapist
and walked to the clinic after school –
slow, and a little ashamed
of my mannish shoes.

i told the boy i loved – a new boy –
that contemplating suicide is something
all imaginative people do just as
all desire is pathological.

    *you are not your body but you are and once it's gone
it's gone.*

and i never saw the point in talking
when truth

is just a sharp thing you stand on in the night, with
    bare feet –
unrepeatable
as a kiss you said

was forced, you never wanted.

dandelion

they're winking in the diphtheric sun
of *bad neighbourhoods*.

the night of my twenty-third birthday i spent
with a coke dealer in a pay-per-hour hotel in Harlem.
a woman at the front desk sold flavoured condoms.

if you listen you find
people open up to you.
you see that pithy coruscating

like a professional in a white mask –

an understanding that you
have no very deep understanding of what
it means *to be human*

but you damn well know you've got to play.

smoker's children

i feel like Jack the Ripper might – hunted
yet wearisomely smug

resigned i will not live to see happy endings
for television's lesbians.

under the eaves of a suburban cafe
making friends with a probable racist
who shares my lighter and disgust
at the necrotic rain –

i don't know why they chose
such a pretty corpse for the packaging. twenty-three,
a stroke, maybe, and a smile that says
he'd do it all again.

is it safe to sleep naked in a hotel room? (a play for voices)

VOICE 1:

i suppose you are concerned with sexually transmitted infections, and have some knowledge of how these are spread from person to person. perhaps this knowledge is first hand. perhaps you yourself have a sexually transmitted infection and are inquiring out of altruism.

VOICE 2:

what you are concerned about is strangers. people you haven't met that have slept or will sleep in this bed. it is fair to assume some people are . . . unclean. the only person whose standards of hygiene we can really be certain are absolutely top-notch, whose standards of hygiene really stand up to scrutiny, are ourselves.

VOICE 3:

or perhaps a lover?

VOICE 2:

no, not even a lover.

VOICE 1:

can absolute trust ever exist between two people?

VOICE 3:

you're talking about solipsism.

VOICE 1:
we're being realistic.

(pause)

to return to the matter at hand, a sexually transmitted infection is unlikely to be passed along via bed linens, even soiled ones. your real worry here is pubic lice. current worldwide prevalence of crab-louse infestation has been estimated at 2% of the population, so it is safe to assume – at this busy hotel, situated in a vibrant international metropolis (with palm trees) – someone with pubic lice has slept in this bed.

VOICE 2:
but were they naked? did they ask if it was safe to sleep naked in this hotel room?

VOICE 4:
it is never safe.

VOICE 1:
non-sexual transmission may occur through shared bed linens. however, the crab louse cannot survive for very long, away from the sustaining warmth of the human body.

VOICE 4:
and who, ultimately, can judge him?

introversion.forum

as if cut from the throat, in the cyan clarity
of the moments that follow intercourse we feel most
   keenly aware
of the ice-cream men and kites snapping taut against the
   wind.

how far below? how many stories up
are we?

ah bonsai.

like a very calm torturer,

laying out my bijou implements
every day.

i think my lover
should be a little tree.

'06

i legitimately want to hear all about the places
you felt like you met god.
that freakout summer

sleeping in the cupboard where they kept the pellet gun
benzene / splinter / abject
upon first hearing.

a good shot
at sixteen, knocking blocks
off a fence-post in denim cutoffs,
a struck bell.

it seems like
everyone who came and went left something,
as if this was a game show —

i wish i could be sure of anything. wish i could tell you
you'll find nothing but encouragement no matter
what dumb shit you want to do.

red sweater

it should take more than one person
to make you want to hang yourself.

i am afraid
i am mistaking what is for what
is good –

it is hard to speak in public,
when that is your covering.

i think of each surface as suitable
for the breaking
of horses, and myself

a lone spine
in glamorous precincts.

★

excuse me, i am
overcome.

a criminal wind sweeps you up –
the end of habit, a part
of love i had.

when i say
come through, come
through.

be there as you were.

i think of you in the darkness
that is routine, and not poetic,
coupling and uncoupling
like magnetic stars.

to think i thought
you had no heart.

but god i really love the world. the things you do.
the way the wind keeps on blowing
without a me to bother.

golem

you tell them not to fuck with you but they'll fuck
with you anyway maybe even fuck you if they can
to give you a real reason to steep your ear in breath
they use to fashion some
apology out of a professed attraction
to 'difficult' women –

Cleopatra was a cunt for going quietly –
carried out by eunuchs to feel the soft rain on her skin.

go down to the river and make a man
with your bare, beautiful hands
and knowledge of sacred geometry.

ensoul.
make him a mouth and spit in it.
learn the only boy worth trusting is your rabbi.

i twitch compulsively

my thoughts return to it in some capacity every day. thereat
i twitch convulsively. i think he is 'good' for staying. then
inducted into the journal: wedding of prominent ethnonationalist figure.
the dream is tinged with schadenfreude as the wedding takes place in a narrow suburban garden,
conditions – driving rain, sky scaled with lead, varicose veins of lighting.

before too long the dream transitions to one of self-castration.
stay with me –

at all moments
i flatter myself i probe the great undisclosed suffering
that smokes cush in the glorious sun. the homeless pussy smell, carpet moths, jackfruit,
drums of cooking oil.

dried spittle on my beard
from where i repeatedly moisten private parts as a form of lonely protest.

sliced at the waist
like an ancient statue, nothing left but to enjoy it anyway.

beau

i have not walked along the Seine –

just by the wharf, between a sun hat

and a body disinterested, finally mature.

after i fell in love his beauty was given to me
like the most destructive secret

and there was never any feeling of having turned a corner.

will the world be so scorched
and conducive to a rarefied survivalism

that they won't understand a life so unsolid, so

centred on
void and plastic?

how i tidy away
the empty blister-pack of his regular bromides

oh how
i feel like god and *endlessly* –

will there still be waterside places people go to die happy?

will they say i was a
lonely seer, a savant, a lover of men?

Acknowledgements

I would like to thank Amy Key, Kate Duckney, Jessica St James, Louis Doyle, Mark Abirached, Edward Caddy, Sophie Collins and Alex MacDonald for their friendship and support. Steffan Blayney and George Vaisey, always. My editors Martha Sprackland and Patrick Davidson Roberts for their assiduous attentions, and the editors of *Clinic 4*, *London Review of Books*, *Poetry London*, *The Poetry Review* and *Test Centre 7*, in which some of these poems originally appeared.

Notes

'my sex': 'Fathers in the Clouds ('99)' is a song by The Magnetic Fields.

'storyboard for a conceptual horror movie': the line 'the front of heaven was full of fiery shapes' is from Shakespeare's Henry IV Part 1.